Ashfall

Ashe

BookLeaf Publishing

India | USA | UK

Made with ❤ on the BookLeaf Publishing Platform
www.bookleafpub.in
www.bookleafpub.com

Dedication

To those who chose to see the lone star
standing amidst the obsidian night sky,

Thank you.

Acknowledgements

For my father, who put my first-ever book in front of me when I was no more than an hour old. For my younger self, thank you for not brushing off any opportunity to pick up a book. To the alphabet for falling into the right places when I needed them the most. To my high school English educator, Tanima Ma'am, who has honestly been more of a friend to me. This is my attempt at apologising to you in advance for only including my poetic melancholia in this one, although let's not disregard the fact that it was you who once said my poems reminded you of Sylvia Plath's. To Richa ma'am, I'll never not carry with me those texts of yours that said, 'Never doubt yourself. 1 conquered, slay the rest too, last main, slay m******.' (I wish I had the guts to uncensor the name, lol). And indeed, 'one conquered', working towards having more to 'slay' so you would not regret having said to me, 'as good as Wordsworth.' To Ms. Mariam

Fatima, my past English teacher, your disdain towards me sparked the matches that lit my fireworks. Your contributions, though unintentional, have failed to go unnoticed, and for that, I'm oddly grateful. But sarcasm apart, I truly am thankful to you for all the times you gave me remarks saying my poems are equally good, if not better, than those we had in our curriculum, as well as all the constructive criticism, which has played a huge part in building my confidence. To Saanvi didi and Harshika didi, I finally got some of my poems published, you guys! Yay! And to my mother, yes, I at last submitted all the required poems.

I also present my gratitude to my cousin, Vihaan, for helping me bring my thoughts to life by editing the book's cover; to Ms. Arpita Mishra for guiding me throughout the process of selecting the illustrations, which without her, would've been an extremely chaotic and time consuming task; and to Tanima Ma'am and Richa Ma'am for writing thoughtful, sublime paragraphs describing the book, along with myself. Lastly, to a certain selectively blinded pedestal-dwelling-figure, who knew intentional invisibility and dismissal could be so creatively empowering?

Preface

In every life, loss is an inevitable visitor – a quiet, uninvited guest that changes everything. It arrives without warning, often leaving behind a trail of sorrow, confusion and longing– a void that words struggle to fill. The poems within these pages are an exploration of that void – the complex, often turbulent journey from the depth of sorrow to the fragile but profound space and quiet clarity of acceptance. Each verse reflects a personal moment, an intimate encounter with the rawness of absence and the gradual, sometimes painful, work of coming to terms with what is no longer. The raw, unfiltered moments of grief, the aching silence of what has been lost and the small, hesitant steps towards healing.

These poems do not promise quick healing or easy answers. They do not offer easy comfort or neat resolutions; rather, they reflect the messy, nonlinear process of learning to live with loss. They do not shy away from the complexity of emotion, nor do they romanticise the pain. Instead, they capture the nuanced, shifting landscape of loss – its sharp edges and tender moments, its rage and silence – and how, over time, it is woven into the fabric of our lives.

As you read, I invite you to sit with these words, to allow the weight of their truth to settle, and, perhaps, to find solace in the shared humanity of loss. For even in the deepest sorrow, there lies the potential for growth, for understanding and ultimately, for acceptance.

This collection is a beginning – a conversation with grief and a testament to the resilience that emerges when we open ourselves to the difficult but necessary work of moving forward. May these poems offer you not only solace but also the recognition that in loss, there is a quiet kind of transformation, and in acceptance, a new way of seeing the world.

vestige.

In a quiet, dusty corner
Are heard echoes of childlike laughters
Faint,
Fleeting,
As they softly linger;
Brushing past,
Cosplaying unseen rafters.
Cobwebbed toys,
Torn pages,
Peeking eyes
Of dreams of younger ages.
Abandoned castles,
Unbuilt towers,

And various others,
Among fading hours.
Walls humming quiet tunes
Recollecting whispered wishes,
Under the crescent moon.
Each corner,
Bearing a tale untold;
Of a mind unburdened,
And a heart brave,
And bold.
All those secrets,
Bound in trust,
Now lie buried beneath
Settling dust.
Time,
A thief?
With a silent tread;
Stole the paths
Where those dreams once led.
Should she dare to kneel, and seek
The voices she hears,
Quite meek.
To lift the veil,
And clear the maroon haze,
In attempt to resurrect,

The golden days.

oblivion.

A garden where wildflowers once bloomed,
Where sunlight flickered
Like a gentle breeze,
And a river's swift flow.
A whole 'nother universe,
Filled with stars,
Twinkling brighter each day
Shimmering constellations,
Concealing all scars.
Each footstep,

Each breath,
Full of life, and love, and joy,
Soon struck by a hurricane,
Turning fresh green grasslands to dusty ashes,
While leaving the flowers in vain.
And before one could feel the effects of
destruction,
The sculptor carved its way through the
smoke,
As the seasons morphed the skies to grey.
Gardens wilted,
Roots turned dry.
The stars,
And their diminishing spotlight in the sky.
The constellations began to fade,
Hidden behind dark clouds.
Leaving the wounds open,
As the audience watched
The
Blood
Bleed
Out.

shards.

'I collect fragments of who I was;
Those that are fallen,
Shattered,
Like broken pieces of glass on the floor.
Sharp edges cutting into the hands that try to
put them together.
Each shard,
Reflecting a different moment,
A different version of who I was,
But they refuse to fit
In the picture frame they've fallen out of,
For when I do put them back in,
None of it feels whole.

So I hold the pieces,
The pieces of the past.
Wondering if it can ever be the same again,
Or if I'll forevermore just be
The mere sum,
Of all that I've lost.'
—autumn

forlorn.

'I've lost parts of myself along the way.
Pieces scattered like forgotten dreams,
Faded voices,
Lost notes,

Dead petals.
All, lost in the spaces between
Glimpses of who I was,
Perhaps,
Who I could've been?
Every now and then,
I look in the drawers of my mind,
Looking for something in particular,
Something I can recognise,
And then being hit by the realisation,
That
That thing is no longer my possessed prize.
All there is left,
Are fragments,
And memories
Of things that no longer fit in.
Things that no longer haunt the chambers of
my conscience.
Yet I still continue to search,
For there is always something that can be
found in the ruins,
Even if
It is just a part of me,
That I thought I'd have lost forever.'
–autumn

unlisted.

She was editing her close friends list on
Instagram,
And she scrolled past your name.
She caught herself
Scrolling
Past
Your
Name.

And she realised that she didn't add you to
her list of close friends anymore.
She stopped;
For a brief moment of incredulity in order to
come to terms with the fact that you and her
are not close friends anymore.
Maybe you two aren't friends at all.
It's intriguing,
How during discussions of love,
Discussions of heartbreak,
It's always centred on romanticism,
While completely neglecting platonic love.
Completely neglecting the thought of
normalising losing a piece of oneself with the
untimely death of a friendship.
The faded laughters,
The comfortable silent whispers.
Now existing, as nothing but mere relics.
For the casket is nothing but an empty void;
An empty void where echoes of old
conversations thrive.
While the grave,
A vast expanse
Where the shadows deployed seem to survive.
Ornamented

With shared memories,
Secrets, even inside jokes.
Yet, the epitaph now bears mere words
Forming an intricate tapestry of what 'was',
Something that has now ceased to exist.

Seemingly the death of them, is quite the
contrary;
For instead, it now marks a new beginning,
For the end of one chapter,
Also means the initiation of another,
Giving room for new friendships to blossom,
While the old ones still continue to whisper.

reverie.

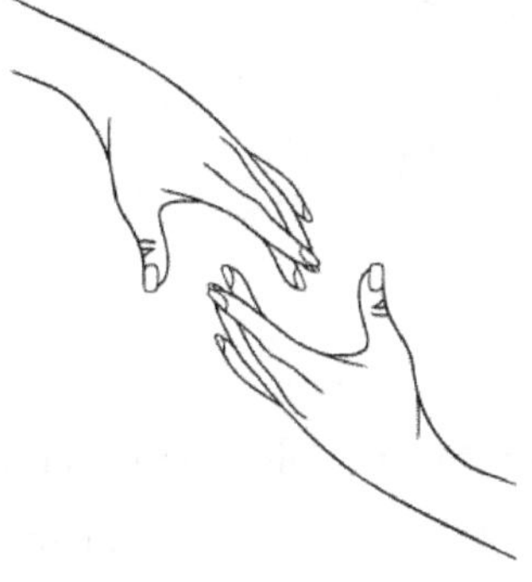

The perfect crime,
Wasn't committed with a knife.
Rather it began,
With what seemed like a harmless smile.

She walked into the coffee shop,
Glancing over her shoulder.
She felt as if time had truly stopped,
The moment he smiled back at her.

They exchanged shy glances,
As days turned to weeks.
They met at the same timings,
When a pink tinge would shadow her cheeks.

Words left unspoken,
Yet truly understood.
While a tale of two hearts,
Silently being brewed.

He'd stir her coffee,
Lost in the other's eyes.
Their conversations bloomed each day,
Like cherry blossoms covering the spring sky.

But beneath the surface of affection,
Were the lurking shadows of a hidden past.
For he carried secrets unspoken,
Dreading to break free at last.

He was a wanderer of distant lands,
Bounded by exile.
Haunted by a love once lost,
While bearing the scars,
At a considerable cost.

Not knowing of his troubled past,
Nor the battles he fought alone.

She continued being the attuned spirit she
was,
Waiting for the love she had always known.

Although it wasn't long,
Before his past caught up.
The whispers of his dark endeavours,
Reached the corners of her ears.

Their stolen moment of bliss,
Barely meant to last a fortnight.
For fate,
Had already entwined its own designs.

For secrets rarely stay concealed,
Like the moon reveals the sun.
The truth too would be revealed,
Causing their love to burn.

So he watched her leave,
Shattered and torn.
As the coffee shop's charm faded,
Like the cardigan,
He'd once worn.

falters.

Tomorrow knocks too early sometimes,
When today hasn't even begun.
Murmurs of moments yet unspoken,
Unwinding like a film reel
Beneath the fiery sun.
Its voice is soft,
Yet relentless.
The clock's hands stretching wide,
Attempting to pull hours from within the
abyss,
Stirring where the night would hide.
Tomorrow knocks too early sometimes,
When today has barely even begun.
Yet the ghost of tomorrow hauntingly lingers,
Receiving
A subtle glance,

A mild shun.
Promises wrapped in a grey haze,
Of dawns unclaimed, and
Brighter days?
The present falters, and flounders, and
quivers,
For it is stretched too thin,
Caught in between all that is,
And all that has been.
Tomorrow knocks too early sometimes,
But now,
Today stands at the horizon.
Whispers heard of
A future radiant and bright?
Is there still room for fear to flourish and
thrive?

knots.

Little tiny fingers fumbled,
Looping laces into messy knots.
One of the first orbs of core memories in her
mind's control panel,
Finally learnt to tie her shoelaces as bows
with careful thoughts.
The bunny ears seemed to dance,
Binding tight,
Holding firm,
As the loops finally found their rhythm.
Years passed;
The same hands now tie different knots each
day.
Only this time,

With threads of decisions,
Twisting,
Tangling,
Through moments
Of doubts,
Resolves,
And untanglings.
The loops now didn't seem quite right,
Made in too much of a rush.
One side too tight,
The other barely holding it all together.
The choices all laced together,
Are they strong enough to carry everything
forward?
Looking back,
There are frayed edges,
Loose ends,
But also knots that refuse to come undone.
Because even if the laces unravel,
Even if they give birth to a stumble,
The path still stretches to infinity,
And the shoes still tread,
Defying everything holding them back, be it
friction, or gravity.
But in the end

A question remains,
Refusing to move on,
Planting seeds of uncertainty;
Is the knot done tight? Or will it soon untie?
'Did I do it right'?

pinned.

She has a Pinterest board
Titled
'Hey Google, play Taylor Swift';
Each pin represents a fragment of the life she
aims to create for herself.
Collages she'd only seen on the internet,
Classic literature she'd never read.
Cities she'd never visited,
And gardens she'd only ever been to in her
head.
Flowers she'd never received,
Museums she'd never seen,
Even no-faced writers

In place of whom she'd pictured herself.
She had pictures of ballgowns and princess'
palaces,
Standing tall and isolated behind enchanted
forests and lakes.
Behind the glossy screen
Was a painted portrait of a life
Which she'd intricately carved with trembling
hands
All stitched together
With ambition weaved between threads.
She watched her cursor hover over each
picture,
Clicking them into place.
As if the universe was constantly listening
And would soon align all of that
In the same space.

fissure.

'Every night,
Between 2:22 a.m. and 3:22 a.m.,
I lose an hour of my life.
It's not daylight savings,
Nor a lapse of time in my dream.
It's swallowed by my thoughts,
Ones that hover over my conscience like
vultures,
Waiting to catch a slight glint of self-doubt.
It consumed me.
My mind.
My reasoning.
My awareness.
I scavenged for it the next morning,
In the sunlight filtering through the cracks
formed between my curtains,

In the chirping of the birds sitting on the
branches of tall trees,
And in the petrichor entering through my
open window.
But it was nowhere to be found.
Gone.
It slipped through my fingers,
The same way my judgement was lost during
that same hour.
But where does it go?
The stolen time of night.
Will I ever reclaim it?
Or will it continue passing through my
fingers as if the gap between them is a slide?
It slips away like sand in an hourglass,
Making it a moment I'm forever destined to
chase.
Or perhaps,
It was never lost in the first place,
Just borrowed by darkness?
Or maybe a trade for something yet unseen,
To see which, maybe some special perceptual
glasses are what I really need.'
–autumn

nostalgia.

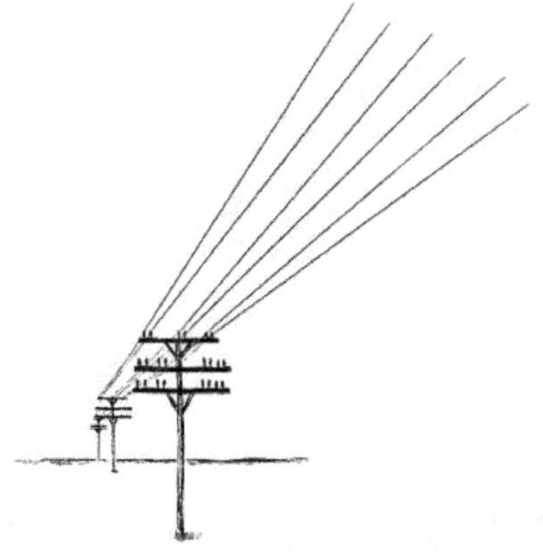

Dusty polaroids
Laying creased on top of piles of cartons,
Those moments,
Strewn in her mind,
Sepia-tinted,
Almost frozen in time.
Echoes of laughter
Still haunting,
Lingering,
In the room long gone,
Those voices,
How could she ever move on?
Nostalgia;

A thief?
A gentle, callous deceiver?
Turning apparitions of loss,
Into illusory altruism.
Although time,
A serene river,
Pulling her forward,
Gradually,
Cautiously,
Reluctantly.
Tides blurring the faces,
Ripples causing the voices to fade,
Like constellations in the night sky,
Hiding,
Slipping right as the sun's rays start to shine.
Yet she strives to hold on,
Quivering,
Grappling,
Trembling,
Holding on
To what?
To when?
Forgetting,
Remembering,
Recalling,

As the past
Precautiously slips through her grasp.
Silence.
The train runs off its tracks,
The rails shaking,
Wheels spinning,
She shuts her eyes,
No clear path ahead in sight.
Yet amidst the chaos,
A scintillating glow,
The moment when she finally dares to let go,
To release,
Not the past,
But the ever tightening pull of its grasp.
And although the echoes still reside,
They seem to leave
Just enough room
To grow,
To breathe,
To be.

keepsakes.

'My favourite sweater got ruined today,
While I was entering my room after coming
back from school the day after my birthday.
The doorknob fell in love with one end of the
thread and refused to let go.
My pulling them apart only seemed to make
it worse.
I attempted to free what was left of my
sweater,
And I did,
But the doorknob still couldn't let go of a
little part of it.
I was upset over the untimely death of my
favourite sweater.
And when I looked back at the doorknob
refusing to let go,

It reminded me of how my sweater stuck by
me through all my most cherished moments,
and more.
I was putting my sweater away,
Safe.
Treasuring all the attached memories to it,
But as I was folding it up,
It struck me how
Life unravelled like the loose threads.
One moment, woven,
The next,
Unkempt.
Each loose weave narrated a story,
How I once hung it the wrong way,
Which birthed a pull in the fabric.
Each worn patch spoke of a time,
When amidst the cold,
It had me wrapped in warmth.
I placed it safely inside a box,
Not as a discarded piece of fabric,
Rather,
A keepsake
Of laughters,
Tears,
And everything in between.

I still take it out sometimes,
To remind myself
That the things we hold on to,
Broken and incomplete
Or not,
Are the ones that hold us together,
When
We try to seek comfort,
And realise that
They're all we got.'
–autumn.

elusive.

'I listen for echoes of the future,
In the ripples of water,
In the rustle of autumn leaves,
And in the hum of distant thunder.
But all I hear is silence.
Voices hiding behind a veil of time.
Appearing to be around the corner,
Yet always just out of reach.
I sometimes receive faint murmurs of voices,
Of things to come,
But they manage to slip through my fingers
like mere gusts of air,
Fading before I'm able to grasp them.
It leaves me in a dilemma.
Is the future always this distant,
Too far out of my reach?

Or is it awaiting my arrival,
For me to finally
Step
Into
It.'
—autumn

traces.

Her life was written on pages
That had been worn out over time,
Written over,
Erased.
But the faint traces remained.
The ink
Holding onto the pages,
Unwilling to let go.
Like the shadows of a bygone day,
Sneaking, lingering in the twilight,
Fading,
Yet refusing to let go.
And the ghost of her past,
Blending in with the new words she wrote.
Her story wasn't clean,
But it was hers.

The fresh ink intertwined with the lingering
shadows of her past.
Each imperfect stroke, deliberate,
Each new chapter unfolding,
Devoid of a clean slate.
The story wasn't pristine,
But the sun's first rays seeped through its
cracks.
The weight of yesterday,
Now a foundation of tomorrow,
A tale unfinished,
Yet undeniably hers to grow.

fractures.

'I threw away years of preserved garbage
today;
Silicon toy organs from when I dreamt of
being a doctor,
Old plastic Barbies covered in crepe
bandages.
It made me realise
How afraid I am to throw away mere garbage,
How afraid I am to throw away mere relics of
who I used to be,
How afraid I am that I'll lose a piece of myself

With each particle I throw away,
Each one representing a fragment of my
childhood.
I lay all alone in my room,
My eyes leaking on my pastel pink satin
pillowcase
As my mind plays reels of reminiscents of the
times when all of that used to be more than
petty garbage;
Old creased papers
With outlines of pink elephants
And sole flowers the size of houses.
Huts, rather.
With pointed triangular mountains in the
background with a sun peeking from behind,
Smiling at the audience.
I rush out of my bedroom,
As I start rummaging through the garbage,
Ferreting out the cartons
In hopes of catching a glimpse of the silicon
organs,
Scrabbling through it all like a raccoon left
loose in a dumpster,
As rivulets contoured my cheekbones,
Descending onto my neck.

I sit there on the floor as my wails fill the
heavy silent air,
Having found nothing but the scent of dust,
As the feeling of my past slips through my
fingers like sand
Tugs on the broken strings of my heart,
As I feel a pull,
A tether,
Fragile,
Fast.
And snap.'
–autumn

haze.

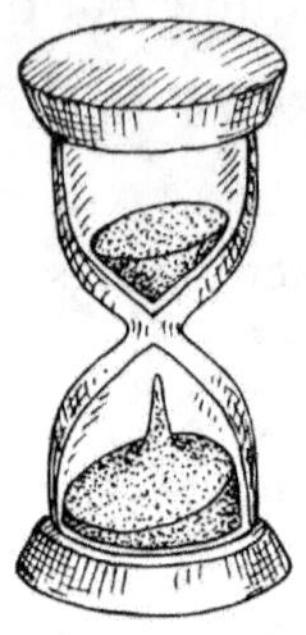

Time has its own way of slipping by right
through the cracks.
Subtle.
Unnoticed.
Subdued.
Like water running through between fingers,
Leaving no marks,
Or signs,
Yet changing everything.
Gradually.
Faintly.
Bit by bit.
Too tenuous to come under perception.
It changes everything.
All that was once clear,

Becomes clouded,
Veiled by the misty grey haze.
The edges of memories start to blur,
Yet the weight of them refuses to leave.
Although
Not all of it as a burden,
Rather,
The breaths that fill
The spaces in between.

mosaic.

Her soul was a mosaic
Of everyone she had ever known.
She wore her scarf the same way her
fifth-grade teacher did,
And tied her hair in braids the way she saw
her favourite influencer do it.
She still wrote lowercase f in cursive the way
her father taught her when she was in the first
grade,
The same tune humming in her head as she
drew the curves to spell the word 'funereal',
One which was etched into her memory like
the faint scent of his cologne.
She always uses one brand of pen to write
with,

For it was the one her best friend suggested to
her when they sat together at the last bench
in sixth grade,
Practicing their signatures for a future they
once dreamed of.
And now
Every word she writes
Carries a piece of those moments.
The clothes she stole from her mother's closet,
Fall on her body the same way they do on her
mother's.
And she's pronounced 'vehicle' differently
since seventh grade,
As her geography teacher's voice still lingers
in her mind, refusing to fade.
She wears her hair in a half-up messy bun the
way she saw her best friend do on their
tenth-grade school trip.
Yet she carries her unchanged personality the
same way her childhood self did.
Each shard of the mosaic,
A memory,
Both jagged,
And smooth.
All come together,

As patches stitched on with time,
Pinned together,
Not always perfect,
The lines didn't always align.
But the spark in her childlike laughter,
Gleaming over the patchwork,
Making it shine,
In ways she could never have thought of.

flickers.

'I was browsing on the internet,
When something caught my eye.
It caused me to stop for a minute,
As it struck me with surprise.
I read as it said,
"Imagine yourself standing in front of your
childhood home
As a little kid comes,
The size of a gnome,
And escorts you, by pulling you in by your
thumb."
You find a place to sit,
As you notice the kid starts crying.
You forbid your mind from entering the pit,

And inquire about what was causing the kid
to worry.
There's no response,
Just sniffles and sobs,
And wails and whimpers.
Gasping for breath in between snivels and
teardrops the size of doorknobs.
You cradle her trembling fear,
Weaving comfort between her cries;
As she thanks you for holding on to dear life?
I did imagine all that;
But my childhood 'home' as the setting, didn't
quite feel right.
For my mind kept drifting away to my
neighbour's house,
While I felt at a loss of might.
Moments later, I saw another post,
One which read,
"Imagine yourself standing somewhere you
feel safe,"
My thoughts immediately welcomed my old
society,
It is then said to imagine yourself looking to
your right and finding a house, at the door of

which a little kid greets you with grace and
instantly catches your sight.
You go in with her,
And find yourself in a room crowded with
different ages of you,
Different versions, different phases
Of you.
The one who was brave enough to follow her
dreams
Sat beside the little girl whose grades never
let her wail or scream.
In front of them,
The burnt-out thirteen-year-old sat,
Holding in her palms, a poem,
One which was lacking a proper format
The heartbroken teen was sitting alone,
For she had let go of the toxic friend
And faced difficulty bearing the cyclone on
her own.
But what failed to catch my attention at the
moment,
Was the coincidence of it being that same
neighbour's home, and,
so the first words to leave your mouth,
"Which one of us is the happiest?"

They all let out a laugh as the eighty-year-old
you state that it's you.
She catches you by surprise but then follows
through by saying how you are exactly where
you are supposed to be,
And not a single thing could make you feel
happier than you already do feel.'
—autumn.

closure.

And finally after three long years,
When the storm within her had settled,
She found it in herself, to move on from the
hatred and try to view beyond the roses;
The ones, black petalled.
She reached out to him.
It consumed everything she had. Everything
she was.
Just to finally admit what she truly felt rather
than the garden of facades she'd convinced
herself of.

And despite the whispers of impending regret
sensed within the quiet chambers of her
intuition, she chose not to step away from the
remorseful flower destined to bloom into the
garden of time
For she would much rather twirl along with
the regret-weaved threads than linger in the
silent waltz of untraversed paths.
For the road 'not' taken will always live to be
a reminder, throwing emphasis over the
negative but 'twas for her to decide how heavy
the reminder could be
When the tale's told,
Somewhere ages and ages hence.
For on the cusp of dawn,
She wishes to say:
'Two roads diverged in a wood, and I–
I took the one less travelled by,
And that has made all the difference.'

pause.

'It's the perfect day to be dead,'
She exclaimed.
'But is it really?'
Inquired her inner voice.
'Have you read all the books you've wanted to
read?
Have you watched all the movies you've
wanted to?
Have you heard all the songs there are that
are just perfect for you?'
Silence filled the air;

'Have you walked down every path you
wished to tread?
Have you met the ones that resemble echoes
of you?
Have you seen the sun rise from every shore?
Have you felt the peace you've always longed
for?'
She stammered,
Hesitantly responding,
'But what if the peace I've sought in the living
world is to be found after death,'
The soliloquy resumed,
'Then before you wish to have yourself erased,
Don't forget to say goodbye
To all the dreams you didn't live to make your
reality.
Say goodbye to running alone at the beach at
twilight.
Say goodbye to whispering secrets to the
night sky under the moonlight.
And say goodbye to blasting songs while
driving with your best friends late at night.'
Her inner monologue went on,
'But just know,

That you are not a name written on a paper
that can be easily erased,
You are a real person with real feelings and
real consequences.
And when you leave,
Will you not wonder about how the sunrise
looked that day or what were the surprise
songs played at your favourite artist's concert
that night?
Will you not wish to rewrite yourself for all
the pain it caused everybody?
But you realise that you can't
And that you are not just a name written in a
chapter in a book on your shelf,
Your name is written in someone else's story
too.
And I'm sorry,
But your story is bigger than you.'

transition.

'There's a void,
Between who I was,
And who I've become.
It is haunted,
By echoes
Of footsteps my feet no longer fit into,
On a path,
I no longer tread.
The chasm's breath carries whispers,
Of the dreams I had once sown,
Of the scars,
The laughters,
That I no longer know.
I turn back,
Staring across the void,
Sharing glances
With a girl I used to know,
With the girl I used to be.
I send her way

A subtle smile.
Her hands lift,
As she waves back,
Responding with a chuckle,
Gleaming with exuberance,
Truly,
A fragile glow.
"Come back!" she yells,
Followed by a delicate whisper of "please."
I turn back,
Unable to look her in the eyes,
For I can't.
I have
grown?
Although I'd love to have her with me,
The path ahead,
Is one I know
I have to tread alone.'
—autumn